AF519809

PREFACE

It is with great pleasure that we present the **CBSE Data Science Class 10 Subject Code: 419 Unsolved Papers (2023 & 2024)**. This compilation is designed to provide students with a valuable resource to aid their preparation for the upcoming board examinations. Data Science is an emerging field that combines various aspects of mathematics, statistics, and computer science to extract meaningful insights from data. As such, it is essential for students to develop a strong foundation in this subject, and practicing past papers is a proven method to enhance their understanding and performance.

The unsolved papers included in this book are official board papers released by CBSE for the years 2023 and 2024. These papers have been curated to reflect the latest trends and patterns in the examination, giving students a clear idea of what to expect on the day of the exam. By working through these papers, students can identify areas where they need improvement, familiarize themselves with the types of questions commonly asked, and develop effective time management strategies.

The primary goal of this book is to encourage self-assessment and critical thinking. We strongly recommend that students attempt these papers under timed conditions, simulating the real exam environment as closely as possible. This approach will not only help in building confidence but also in honing the skills required to tackle the examination successfully.

We have taken great care to ensure that the content of this book is accurate and aligned with the CBSE curriculum. The questions are arranged in a manner that allows for progressive learning, starting from basic concepts and gradually moving towards more complex topics. This structure is intended to help students strengthen their knowledge base while also challenging them to think critically and analytically.

As you embark on your journey of preparation, we hope that this book serves as a reliable companion and a valuable tool in your academic success. Remember, consistent practice and a clear understanding of concepts are key to excelling in Data Science. We wish you all the best in your studies and in your forthcoming examinations.

Table of Contents

CBSE PREVIOUS YEAR QUESTION PAPER 2023

SUBJECT CODE: 419

SET-4

Q.P. CODE: 106

Instructions:

1. Please check that this question paper contains **21** questions.
2. Q.P. Code given on the right-hand side of the question paper should be written on the title page of the answer-book by the candidate.
3. Please write down the serial number of the question in the answer-book before attempting it.
4. 15-minute time has been allotted to read this question paper. The question paper will be distributed at 10.15 a.m. From 10.15 a.m. to 10.30 a.m., the students will read the question paper only and will not write any answer on the answer-book during this period.

DATA SCIENCE

Time allowed: 2 hours **Maximum Marks: 50**

General Instructions:

1. Please read the instructions carefully.
2. This question paper consists of 21 questions in two sections: Section A and Section B.
3. Section A has Objective Type Questions, whereas Section B contains Subjective Type Questions.
4. Out of the given (5 + 16 =) 21 questions, the candidate has to answer (5 + 10 =) 15 questions in the allotted (maximum) time of 2 hours.
5. All questions of a particular section must be attempted in the correct order.
6. Section A: Objective Type Questions (24 marks):

a. This section has 5 questions.

b. There is no negative marking.

c. Do as per the instructions given.

d. Marks allotted are mentioned against each question/part.

7. Section B: Subjective Type Questions (26 marks):

a. This section has 16 questions.

b. A candidate has to do 10 questions.

c. Do as per the instructions given.

Marks allotted are mentioned against each question/part.

SECTION A

(Objective Type Questions) (24 marks)

1. Answer any 4 out of the given 6 questions on Employability Skills. (4 1=4)

(i) Stress management can help you to

a. have a joyful life.

b. have a stressful life.

c. be less energetic.

d. have no time for friends and family.

(ii) Which type of motivation makes us do things because they make us happy?

a. Internal motivation

b. External motivation

c. Both (a) and (b)

d. Neither (a) nor (b)

(iii) Which of the following is a mobile operating system?

a. Ubuntu

b. Microsoft Windows

c. Google Android

d. macOS

(iv) Installing the ________ helps in increasing the performance of the computer.

a. spam files

b. disk cleaner software

c. temporary files

d. extra files

(v) Making decisions is an important of ________ an entrepreneur.

a. Misconception

b. hindrance

c. function

d. myth

(vi) A/An ________ is a line of work that a person takes for life.

a. Impression

b. commission

c. quality

d. career

2. Answer any 5 out of the given 6 questions. (5 X 1=5)

(i) State whether the following statement is true or false:

Subsetting helps to focus first on the required set of data.

(ii) Which of the following statement is true about median?

a. It is the smallest element of a sorted data set.

b. It is the middle point of a sorted data set.

c. It is the middle point of an unsorted data set.

d. It is the smallest element of an unsorted data set.

(iii) Standard Deviation represents how much the data is spread out around the ______________ or an average.

a. Standard deviation

b. Mean deviation

c. Mean

d. Median

(iv) Two-way relative frequency tables represent the percentage of _______ that fit in each category.

a. Preference

b. data points

c. mean values

d. frequency

(v) ________ is an example of discrete data.

a. Pass or Fail in a Math Test

b. Length of a road

c. Weather forecast

d. Number of stars

(vi) Which of the following is not true for discarding the data?

a. This helps us to prevent unauthorized access to the data.

b. It is important for all of us to make sure that we discard the digital data in a proper way.

c. In most of the devices, if you do a soft delete of a particular file, this file deletes from the original space and cannot be restored.

d. With the increased amount and intensity of cyber-attacks, it is important for all of us to make sure that we discard the digital data in a proper way.

3. Answer any 5 out of the given 6 questions. (5 X 1=5)

(i) Data Merging is the process of combining two or more data sets into a single ______. .

a. Data Frame

b. Data Designing

c. Data Graphing

d. Data Handling

(ii) ______bias is an outcome of seeing what you want to see in the data.

a. Linearity

b. Selection

c. Survivor

d. Confirmation

(iii) ______is all about counting randomness.

a. Mean

b. Median

c. Probability

d. Graphs

(iv) ______is an example of real-life implementation of standard deviation.

a. Grading tests

b. Sum of values

c. Sorting of data

d. Spellcheck

(v) The private information that is shared should ______be handled with confidentiality.

a. never

b. sometimes

c. always

d. often

(vi) There are two ways in which you can store the data in the __________ format or as a physical copy.

a. analog

b. printed

c. hardcopy

d. digital

4. Answer any 5 out of the given 6 questions. (5 1=5)

(i) A percentile can be defined as the percentage of the total ordered observations at or __________it.

a. above

b. equal

c. below

d. not at

(ii) The value of a z-score always tells us the number of standard deviations we are away from___________.

a. median

b. mean

c. standard deviation

d. percentile

(iii) One-to-one join works by ___________ the data tables using the Primary key.

a. merging

b. deleting

c. inserting

d. concatenating

(iv) Which of the following is true about distribution of an event?

a. It shows no values.

b. It consists of only input values that can be seen.

c. It consists of all possible values but not input values.

d. It consists of both input values that can be seen and also all possible values.

(v) Which of the following is the last step of the Statistical Problem-Solving Process?

a. Analyse the data

b. Formulate statistical investigative questions

c. Interpret the data

d. Collect the data

(vi) Which of the following is used to find out the interquartile range?

a. Values of quartiles

b. Values of percentiles

c. Values of deciles

d. Values of z-score

5. Answer any 5 out of the given 6 questions. (5 X 1=5)

(i) The weight of students in a class has a mean of 22 with standard deviation of 4. What is the z-score for a student who weighs 30 kg?

a. 0

b. 1

c. 2

d. 3

(ii) The median of the given dataset values 7, 12, 15, 16, 20 is

a. 15

b. 10

c. 11

d. 12

(iii) The mean absolute deviation for the data 3, 5, 9, 10, 15, 16 is

a. 5

b. 3

c. 4

d. 6

(iv) If two coins are tossed at the same time, what is the probability of getting Head-Tail?

a. 0.50

b. 0.45

c. 0.25

d. 0.35

(v) Data collection designs must acknowledge ___________ in data.

a. Statistical Process Control

b. Test Data

c. Variability

d. Experimental Designs

(vi) If the data that is fed into the system is ___________model accuracy and fidelity are compromised.

a. biased

b. predictive

c. accurate

d. continuous

SECTION B

(Subjective Type Questions) **(26 marks)**

Answer any 3 out of the given 5 questions on Employability Skills. Answer each question in 20 – 30 words. ***(3×2=6)***

1. What is self-motivation? Give an example.

2. Explain any two steps for Effective Time Management.

3. Define any two of the following:

a. Virus

b. Identity Theft

c. Software Piracy

4. What are the two ways of employment in which one can earn a living? Give an example for each.

5. What are the qualities of an entrepreneur?

Answer any 4 out of the given 6 questions in 20 - 30 words each. **(4 X 2=8)**

6. What is Data-based subsetting? Give an example.

7. What is Continuous data? Give an example.

8. Why is Central Limit Theorem important?

9. What is Many-to-Many Join? Give an example to support your answer.

10. Name the two ways in which data can be stored. Give an example.

11. Define the term percentile. Give an example.

Answer any 3 out of the given 5 questions in 50 - 80 words each. **(3 X 4=12)**

12. Give the steps to calculate Standard Deviation.

13. Explain the following components of the Statistical Problem-Solving Process with example:

a. Formulate statistical investigative questions

b. Collect/Consider the data

14. Differentiate between Recall Bias and Survivor Bias. Give an example of each.

15. What is the Interquartile Range? Give an example to calculate an interquartile range.

16. Mention any two ways to discard the data stored in physical copy and any two ways to discard digital data.

CBSE PREVIOUS YEAR QUESTION PAPER 2024

SUBJECT CODE: 419

SET-4

Q.P. CODE: 106

Instructions:

1. Please check that this question paper contains 21 questions.
2. Q.P. Code given on the right-hand side of the question paper should be written on the title page of the answer-book by the candidate.
3. Please write down the serial number of the question in the answer-book before attempting it.
4. 15 minutes have been allotted to read this question paper. The question paper will be distributed at 10.15 a.m. From 10.15 a.m. to 10.30 a.m., the students will read the question paper only and will not write any answer on the answer-book during this period.

DATA SCIENCE

Time allowed: 2 hours **Maximum Marks: 50**

General Instructions:

1. Please read the instructions carefully.
2. This question paper consists of 21 questions in two sections: Section A and Section B.
3. Section A has Objective Type Questions, whereas Section B contains Subjective Type Questions.
4. Out of the given (5 + 16 =) 21 questions, the candidate has to answer (5 + 10 =) 15 questions in the allotted (maximum) time of 2 hours.
5. All questions of a particular section must be attempted in the correct order.
6. Section A: Objective Type Questions (24 marks):

a. This section has 5 questions.

b. There is no negative marking.

c. Do as per the instructions given.

d. Marks allotted are mentioned against each question/part.

7. Section B: Subjective Type Questions (26 marks):

a. This section has 16 questions.

b. A candidate has to do 10 questions.

c. Do as per the instructions given.

Marks allotted are mentioned against each question/part.

SECTION A

(Objective Type Questions) (24 marks)

1. Answer any 4 out of the given 6 questions on Employability Skills. (4X1=4)

(i) What is a common misconception about starting a business?

a. You need a large amount of money to get started

b. Starting a business requires no financial investment

c. You can start a business with whatever money you have

d. Every business idea has to be unique

(ii) Which of the following is not true with respect to self-awareness abilities?

a. Being self-aware means that you can identify your strengths and weaknesses.

b. Self-awareness helps to convert your strength to weakness.

c. Self-awareness helps to convert your strength to exceptional talent.

d. Analysing your strengths and weaknesses helps you to attain success in life.

(iii) Managing   is about making a plan to be able to cope effectively with daily pressures and to strike a balance between life, work, relationships, relaxation, and fun.

a. Weight

b. Stress

c. Beliefs

d. Interests

(iv) Which of the following is a type of verbal communication?

a. Gestures

b. Body language

c. Facial expressions

d. Interpersonal communication

(v) What is the keyboard shortcut for copying selected text or files in most operating systems?

a. Ctrl + X

b. Ctrl + Z

c. Ctrl + V

d. Ctrl + C

(vi) How many Sustainable Development Goals (SDGs) were adopted by the United Nations in 2015?

a. 5

b. 10

c. 15

d. 17

2. Answer any 5 out of the given 6 questions. (5X1=5)

(i) In data analysis, why should you create subsets of your data?

a. To increase the size of your dataset

b. To make the data easier to analyse

c. To add extra information in your dataset

d. To add noise to the data

Which of the following graphs shows the probability distribution for tossing a coin?

a. 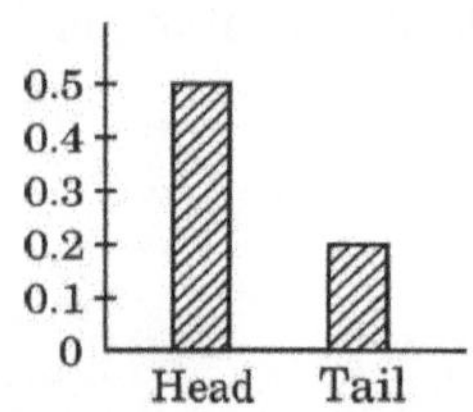

b. 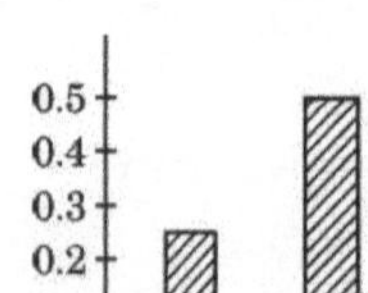

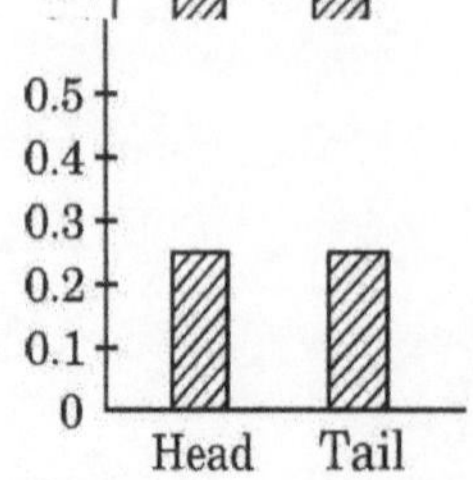

c.

d. 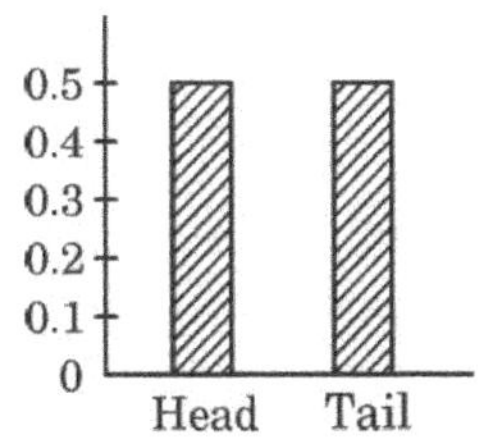

(i) In Data Science, ________________________ is a deviation from the expected outcome in the data.

a. Outlier

b. Standard Deviation

c. Bias

d. Variance

(ii) Identify the type of join from the following diagram.

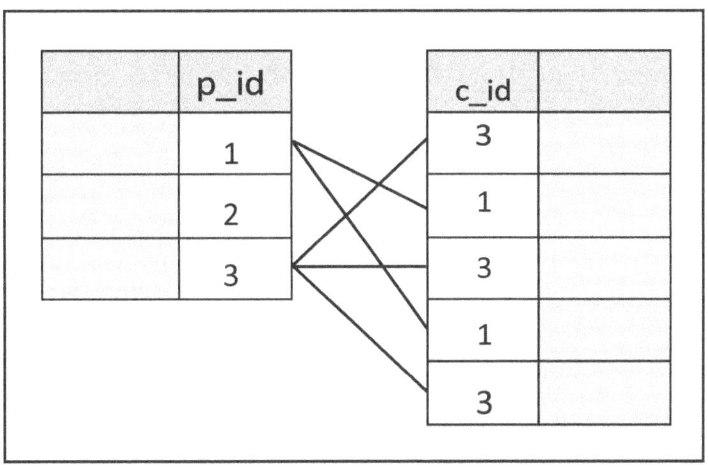

a. Many to Many

b. One to Many

c. One to One

d. Many to One

(iii) State True or False.

If you soft delete a particular file, it gets deleted permanently and cannot be restored.

(iv) Statement I: Shredding and cutting are two ways to discard physical data.

Statement II: The shredded documents can be read easily but the documents that are cut down into small pieces cannot be read.

a. Both statement I and Statement II are true

b. Both statement I and Statement II are false

c. Statement I is true, but Statement II is false

d. Statement II is true, but Statement I is false

2. Answer any *5* out of the given *6* questions. ***(5×1=5)***

(i) A ________ table represents the percentage of data points that fit in each category.

a. Dummy

b. Two-way frequency

c. Two-way relative frequency

d. Two-way direct frequency

(ii) The value of z-score is always ________ if the value of z-score lies above the mean.

a. Positive

b. Negative

c. Zero

d. Infinite

(iii) What does a distribution represent in Data Science?

a. The exact values for a variable and how often they occur

b. The probable values for a variable and how often they occur

c. The average values for a variable and how often they occur

d. The maximum values for a variable and how often they occur

(iv) In which bias do we assume that change in one quantity produces an equal and proportional change in another?

a. Linearity Bias

b. Confirmation Bias

c. Recall Bias

d. Selection Bias

(v) Which of the following is an appropriate way of discarding physical copies of confidential data?

a. Crumbing the papers which contain confidential data and throwing them in the dustbin

b. Burning the documents

c. Leaving the confidential data in an unlocked drawer

d. Using the papers containing confidential data for rough work.

(vi) Quartiles of a dataset partition the data in _________ equal parts.

a. Three

b. Four

c. Six

d. Eight

3. Answer any 5 out of the given 6 questions. (5 X 1=5)

(vii) What security measure should you employ to ensure that even in the case of a data leak, the hackers are not able to read your data ?

a. Backing up data to an external drive

b. Using any password

c. Encrypting the data

d. Deleting the data

(viii) In a dataset of income levels for a small town's residents, the income data includes a few extremely high values (outliers) due to the presence of some wealthy individuals. In the scenario, which form of central tendency would be more appropriate to describe the typical income of the town's residents?

a. Mean

b. Median

c. Mode

d. Range

(ix) What is the correct order of steps in the Statistical Problem Solving Process?

a. Collect/Consider the data, formulate statistical investigative questions, Analyse the data, Interpret the results

b. Analyse the data, Interpret the results, Collect/Consider the data, Formulate statistical investigative questions

c. Formulate statistical investigative questions, Collect/Consider the data, Interpret the results, Analyse the data

d. Formulate statistical investigative questions, Collect/Consider the data, Analyse the data, Interpret the results

(x) If n is the total number of data in a sample, which of the following correctly represents the first decile?

a. D1 = 1 * (n+1) / 10th Data

b. D1 = 1 + (n+1) / 10th Data

c. D1 = 1 (n+1) / 10th Data

d. D1 = 1 / (n+1) / 10th Data

(xi) If you have a dataset with 100 data points, what data point defines the first quartile (Q1)?

a. The 25th percentile

b. The 50th percentile

c. The 75th percentile

d. The 100th percentile

(xii) Which type of bias is commonly associated with recommendation systems, polls, and personalised advertisements, where the sample data is not representative of the true future population of cases that the model will see?

a. Linearity Bias

b. Recall Bias

c. Selection Bias

d. Survivor Bias

2. Answer any 5 out of the given 6 questions. (5 X 1=5)

(i) Statement I: In Data Science, we can perform data merging by implementing data joins on the databases in frame.

Statement II: There are five categories of data joins.

a. Both statement I and statement II are correct

b. Both statement I and statement II are incorrect

c. Statement I is correct, but statement II is incorrect

d. Statement I is incorrect, but statement II is correct

(ii) You have a dataset of ages for a group of 5 people. The ages are as follows: 25, 32, 29, 35 and 27. What is the median age for this dataset?

a. 27

b. 28

c. 29

d. 30

(iii) You have a bag with two red marbles and two green marbles. If you randomly select one marble from the bag without looking, what is the probability that it will be a red marble?

a. 0·50

b. 0·25

c. 1·0

d. 0·75

(iv) In statistical analysis, what minimum sample size is generally considered enough for the Central Limit Theorem to hold?

a. 5

b. 10

c. 20

d. 30

(v) Deciles sort the data into how many equal parts?

a. 5

b. 10

c. 9

d. 8

(vi) Assertion (A): Privacy does not always mean confidentiality of data.

Reason (R): Private data may need to be audited based on the relevant requirements.

a. Both (A) and (R) are correct and (R) is the correct explanation of (A).

b. Both (A) and (R) are correct, but (R) is not the correct explanation of (A).

c. (A) is correct, but (R) is incorrect.

d. (R) is correct, but (A) is incorrect.

SECTION B

(Subjective Type Questions) (26 marks)

Answer any 3 out of the given 5 questions on Employability Skills. Answer each question in 20 – 30 words. ***(3×2=6)***

1. Give any two ways to overcome barriers of effective communication.

2. Differentiate between wage employed people and self-employed people.

3. Explain any two key strategies or initiatives that can contribute towards achieving Sustainable Development Goals (SDGs).

4. Define any two of the following terms:

a. ICT

b. Trojan horse

c. Firewall

5. What does the acronym SMART stand for in the context of goal setting? Why is goal setting an essential factor in your personal life?

Answer any 4 out of the given 6 questions in 20 - 30 words each. (4 X 2=8)

6. Discuss any two ways of protecting confidential data that is stored in digital form.

7. Write steps to calculate Mean Absolute Deviation (MAD).

8. Explain the concept of Recall Bias in Statistics.

9. For each of the following scenarios, classify the data as either discrete or continuous:

a. Result of an admission test

b. Weight of apples at a grocery store

c. Football score in a match

d. Depth of a river

10. Explain one-to-one join with the help of an example.

11. In a dataset representing the ages of a group of people, the lower quartile (Q1) is 30 years, and the upper quartile (Q3) is 50 years. Calculate the interquartile range (IQR) for this dataset.

Answer any 3 out of the given 5 questions in 50 - 80 words each. (3 X 4=12)

12. What is a two-way frequency table? Explain its features with a suitable example.

13. Explain the following components of the Statistical Problem Solving Process:

a. Analyse the data

b. Interpret the results

14. Explain Central Limit Theorem. Give any two real world scenarios in which it is used.

15. What is z-score in data science? Write the formula to calculate z-score. Also explain the importance of z-score in data science.

16. You are a data analyst working for a healthcare organisation. Your team is responsible for analysing patient data to improve healthcare services and outcomes. Ethical considerations are crucial in handling this sensitive information. Recently, you received a dataset containing patient records, including medical history, personal information, and treatment details.

(i) What is the most important ethical consideration when handling patient's data?

a. Data accuracy and quality

b. Data sharing with external organisations without patients knowledge

c. Data storage cost optimisation

d. Patient's privacy protection

(ii) A colleague suggests using patient's data to train an artificial intelligence model without the patients consent. What is your ethical stance on this suggestion?

a. Support the idea as it can lead to technological advancements

b. Implement the idea without informing the patients

c. Reject the idea and ensure patient consent is obtained for any data usage

d. Share the colleague's idea with other organisations for wider adoption

(iii) List any two ethical guidelines around data analysis.

CBSE PREVIOUS YEAR QUESTION PAPER 2025

SUBJECT CODE: 419

SET-4

Q.P. CODE: 106

Instructions:

Please check that this question paper contains **21** questions.

Q.P. Code given on the right-hand side of the question paper should be written on the title page of the answer-book by the candidate.

Please write down the serial number of the question in the answer-book before attempting it.

15-minute time has been allotted to read this question paper. The question paper will be distributed at 10.15 a.m. From 10.15 a.m. to 10.30 a.m., the students will read the question paper only and will not write any answer on the answer-book during this period.

DATA SCIENCE

Time allowed: 2 hours **Maximum Marks: 50**

General Instructions:

1. Please read the instructions carefully.
2. This question paper consists of **21** questions in **two** sections: **Section A** and **Section B**.
3. Section A has Objective Type Questions, whereas Section B contains Subjective Type Questions.
4. **Out of the given (5 + 16 =) 21 questions, the candidate has to answer (5 + 10 =) 15 questions in the allotted (maximum) time of 2 hours.**
5. All questions of a particular section must be attempted in the correct order.
6. **Section A**: Objective Type Questions (24 marks):
   a. This section has **5** questions.
   b. There is no negative marking.

c. Do as per the instructions given.

d. Marks allotted are mentioned against each question/part.

7. **Section B**: Subjective Type Questions (26 marks):

a. This section has **16** questions.

b. A candidate has to do **10** questions.

c. Do as per the instructions given.

d. Marks allotted are mentioned against each question/part.

SECTION A

(Objective Type Questions) (24 Marks)

1. Answer any *4* out of the given *6* questions on Employability Skills. (4X1=4)

(i) Which of the following is *not* true for communication?

(A) The receiver transmits the message through one medium or another.

(B) The receiver listens or understands the message.

(C) The receiver conveys his/her understanding of the message to the sender in the form of feedback to complete the communication cycle.

(D) The word 'communication' comes from the Latin word commūnicāre, meaning 'to share'.

(ii) Having the ability to work independently means ___________.

(A) not accepting mistakes

(B) stop learning after a certain point

(C) becoming self-aware, self-monitoring and self-correcting

(D) blaming others for the slightest mistake

(iii) __________ is our ability to do the things that need to be done without someone or something influencing us.

(A) Self-management (B) Self-motivation

(C) Self-control (D) Self-care

(iv) __________ are computer programs that can damage the data and software programs or steal the information stored on a computer.

(A) Viruses (B) Theft

(C) Antivirus (D) BIOS

(v) __________ is the type of self-employment where one is running a business to satisfy the needs of people and looking for ways to make the business better to make profits.

(A) Wage employment

(B) Services

(C) Creativity

(D) Entrepreneurship

(vi) __________ is the development that satisfies the needs of the present without compromising the capacity of future generations, guaranteeing the balance between economic growth, care for the environment and social well-being.

(A) Sustainable development

(B) Economic development

(C) Personal development

(D) Global development

2. Answer any *5* out of the given *6* questions. (*5* X *1*=*5*)

(i) The median is the middle point of a/an __________ data set.

(A) Unsorted (B) Sorted

(C) Grouped (D) Labelled

(ii) What does a distribution represent in Data Science?

(A) A method which shows the probable values for a variable and how often they occur.

(B) It is the measure of how spread out the numbers are.

(C) It is the average of how far away all values in a data set are from the mean.

(D) The maximum values for a variable and how often they occur.

(iii) Confirmation Bias is also known as __________.

(A) Recall Bias

(B) Selection Bias

(C) Observer Bias

(D) Linearity Bias

(iv) In Data Science, __________ is the process of combining two or more data sets into a single data frame.

(A) Pattern (B) Data merging

(C) Distribution (D) Probability

(v) ___________ does not always mean confidentiality because private data may need to be audited based on the relevant requirements.

(A) Privacy

(B) Data governance

(C) Ethical guidelines

(D) Bias

(vi) State True or False :

The private data acquired from a person with their consent should be exposed for use by different businesses or individuals.

3. Answer any *5* out of the given *6* questions. *(5 X 1=5)*

(i) While interpreting two-way tables, categories are placed in _________ column and __________ row.

(A) bottom, right (B) top, left

(C) top, right (D) bottom, left

(ii) The statistical problem-solving process involves mainly __________ component(s).

(A) One (B) Two

(C) Three (D) Four

(iii) Assertion (A) : Biased models tend to discriminate against certain groups of people.

Reason (R) : It is very important to eliminate the bias to avoid these risks.

(A) Both Assertion (A) and Reason (R) are true and Reason (R) is the correct explanation of Assertion (A).

(B) Both Assertion (A) and Reason (R) are true, but Reason (R) is *not* the correct explanation of Assertion (A).

(C) Assertion (A) is true, but Reason (R) is false.

(D) Assertion (A) is false, but Reason (R) is true.

(iv) ___________ is also known as standard score as it allows comparison of scores on different types of variables by standardizing the distribution.

(A) Joins

(B) Z-Score

(C) Percentiles

(D) Distribution

(v) The one-to-one join works by merging the data tables using the __________ key.

(A) Basic

(B) Secondary

(C) Primary

(D) Alternate

(vi) The private information that is shared should always be handled ____________.

(A) Irresponsibly

(B) with Confidentiality

(C) Emotionally

(D) Carelessly

4. Answer any *5* out of the given *6* questions. *(5X1=5)*

(i) In Data Science, what is a subset ?

(ii) Distribution in statistics is defined by underlying ___________ and not by the graph.

(A) Probabilities (B) Median

(C) Mean (D) Analysis

(iii) The __________ states that the distribution of sample mean nears normal distribution as the sample size gets bigger.

(A) Probability

(B) Central Limit Theorem

(C) Identifying Patterns

(D) Distribution

(iv) The Z-Score is always __________ if the value of Z-Score lies above the mean and it is _________ if its value is below the mean.

(A) Positive, Negative

(B) Negative, Positive

(C) Positive, Zero

(D) Negative, Zero

(v) A/An __________ can be defined as the measure of the middle 50% of the values when ordered from lowest to highest.

(A) Percentile

(B) Quartile

(C) Interquartile range

(D) Z-Score

(vi) Data should institutionalize unfair means. (True/False)

5. Answer any *5* out of given *6* questions. (*5*X*1*=*5*)

(i) Mean is a measure of central tendency. (True/False)

(ii) Depth of an ocean, weight of a person or length of a road are examples of __________ data.

(A) Discrete (B) Qualitative

(C) Fixed (D) Continuous

(iii) We can use ____________ to predict how likely or unlikely particular events may be.

(A) Distribution

(B) Probability

(C) Partiality

(D) Random Experiment

(iv) The mathematical formula for calculating the Z-Score is Z = (x – y)/y, where x = raw score, X = mean.

What does X stand for ?

(A) Standard Deviation

(B) Median

(C) Distribution

(D) Percentile

(v) A __________ can be defined as the percentage of the total ordered observations at or below it.

(A) Standard Deviation

(B) Percentile

(C) Mean

(D) Median

(vi) Once we are done with the user data, especially confidential data, it is important that we ___________ this data.

(A) Sell (B) Misuse

(C) Discard (D) Forward

SECTION B

(Subjective Type Questions) (26 Marks)

Answer any 3 out of the given 5 questions based on Employability Skills in 20 – 30 words each. (3X2=6)

6. What is Interpersonal Communication? Give an example to explain it.

7. List any four stress management techniques.

8. What is the purpose of an antivirus software?

9. "A person needs a lot of money to start a business."

Is this statement a fact or myth ? Justify your answer.

10. Briefly discuss any two major problems related to Sustainable Development.

Answer any 4 out of the given 6 questions in 20 – 30 words each. (4X2=8)

11. What is Standard Deviation? Give an example

12. Briefly explain the term Discrete Data with the help of an example.

13. What is Recall Bias? Why does it occur?

14. Why is the Z-score so important? Give any two key points.

15. What is One-to-many Join? Give an example to support your answer.

16. While safely discarding the physical copies of confidential data, mention any one situation in which cutting the documents into pieces is considered an appropriate method. Also mention any one point to consider while cutting the documents into pieces to ensure the successful discarding of the data.

Answer any 3 out of the given 5 questions in 50 – 80 words each. (3X4=12)

17. List down the steps to find standard deviation.

18. What is Uniform distribution? Make a probability table for tossing two coins.

19. With reference to Data Science, answer the following questions:

(a) What is Bias?

(b) Why does it occur?

(c) Why is it important to eliminate the Bias? Discuss in detail.

20. List down the steps to calculate decile.

21. Explain the need and ways to discard digital data.

ADDITIONAL RESOURCES

Videos

CLASS 10th Videos Playlist

Link:

https://www.youtube.com/playlist?list=PLzlh_31VWEFoVqTp4znpXOoWrT-cVwWMW

QR Code:

Exam Last Hour Review Questions Playlist Video

Link:

https://www.youtube.com/playlist?list=PLzlh_31VWEFrAuXqOQkh3-gvxGo1mf1m7

QR Code:

Annual Test Papers Exam Practises

Sample Paper I

Link: https://forms.office.com/r/rWMcnxW5PF

QR Code:

Sample Paper II

Link: https://forms.office.com/r/YQQdNbzfes

QR Code:

Sample Paper III

Link: https://forms.office.com/r/kCFQq40QRz

QR Code:

Sample Paper IV

Link: https://forms.office.com/r/JWwpZ29mZQ

QR Code:

Sample Paper V

Link: https://forms.office.com/r/uGuQtSnDqx

QR Code:

YouTube Videos Playlists for all Chapters

Chapter 1

Link:

https://www.youtube.com/playlist?list=PLzlh_31VWEFp4J4UOCFVbsIDPo0OsJNDX

QR Code:

Chapter 2

Link: https://www.youtube.com/playlist?list=PLzlh_31VWEFp8h4Q708212s_VJ6T1Z7p-

QR Code:

Chapter 3

Link: https://www.youtube.com/playlist?list=PLzlh_31VWEFrtqSK8wS3q9P46EdrhvuqS

QR Code:

Chapter 4

Link:

https://www.youtube.com/playlist?list=PLzlh_31VWEFpG3KKpNVamdN593C-jXaXy

QR Code:

Chapter 5

Link:

https://www.youtube.com/playlist?list=PLzlh_31VWEFqiNmnP8AB7vcoRgcNmTQpD

QR Code:

Chapter 6

Link: https://www.youtube.com/playlist?list=PLzlh_31VWEFrYIzRyJT3t1684R4Y6eLkm

QR Code:

Chapter 7

Link:

https://www.youtube.com/playlist?list=PLzlh_31VWEFp_wKlb9hGMAkkMDMxWOGpn

QR Code:

Chapter 8

Link: https://www.youtube.com/playlist?list=PLzlh_31VWEFr6v5XceXr3Een0UqYakky2

QR Code:

Chapter 9

Link: https://www.youtube.com/playlist?list=PLzlh_31VWEFpjV17QeFDfsqAeJXmeyV-5

QR Code:

Chapter 10

Link:

https://www.youtube.com/playlist?list=PLzlh_31VWEFpHkH8vfUXauLp_P0er8HN5

QR Code:

Chapter 11

Link: https://www.youtube.com/playlist?list=PLzlh_31VWEFp764-2lTn-qRL_5mz5iwiD

QR Code:

Chapter 12

Link:

https://www.youtube.com/playlist?list=PLzlh_31VWEFoB4k8IomqfSy8KboMO03IW

QR Code:

Chapter 13

Link: https://www.youtube.com/playlist?list=PLzlh_31VWEFpb5S4aGdABgoQlv1cL0aXp

QR Code: